Dreaming of France

Kerry Tepperman Campbell

BLUE LIGHT PRESS ◆ 1ST WORLD PUBLISHING

1ST WORLD
PUBLISHING

SAN FRANCISCO ◆ FAIRFIELD ◆ DELHI

WINNER OF THE 2017 BLUE LIGHT BOOK AWARD

Dreaming of France

Copyright ©2018 by Kerry Tepperman Campbell

1st World Library
PO Box 2211
Fairfield, IA 52556
www.1stworldpublishing.com

Blue Light Press
www.bluelightpress.com
Email: bluelightpress@aol.com

Book & Cover Design
Melanie Gendron
www.melaniegendron.com

First Edition
ISBN 9781421837840
Library of Congress Control Number: 2017954091

All rights reserved. Printed in the United States of America. No part of this book may be used or reproduced in any manner whatsoever without written permission except in the case of brief quotations embodied in critical articles and reviews.

In memory of my friend Jacqui Fairborn,
who once created a patchwork cowboy shirt
for the French artist Jean Dubuffet

CONTENTS

III

Dreaming of France

pleached

trees planted so close their branches
entwine and sometimes grow together; pleached
trees form thickets, bowers, and canopies

DREAMING OF FRANCE

Perhaps a woman dreams, and the woman she dreams of dreams of another woman. Then perhaps one of these women dreams of a fox, or a bird, or an open window, or a folding screen in a Paris atelier with the face of a woman painted on each panel.

Or perhaps it is not a dream. Perhaps a woman imagines a gold clasp, or a ruby mouth, or a clearing near Arles where night folds in on itself.

In this clearing, within the folded darkness, perhaps an accordion is being played by a snake. Its coiled body squeezing the instrument, in, out. Its head and tail sauntering up and down the keys, a snake dreaming it is a woman with hair and fingers and a feathered ball gown, a snake yearning to put its whole back into that gown.

Or perhaps it is simpler than that. Perhaps a woman dreams she is grooming her eyebrows, or whisking egg whites, or sewing on a button.

Or perhaps it is even less complicated. Perhaps a woman simply catches a glimpse of herself in a store window when she is alone for a moment between destinations.

THE CHARACTERS, THE DREAMERS, SHE

The characters are various women who dream about France.

These women, these dreamers, are all American, although some may have a French parent, or French grandparents, or live in France, or travel there frequently.

All of them dream about France, although some of them imagine, and some remember and, sometimes, dream and memory and imagination intertwine.

Each dreamer is distinct from the others, but not distinct.

Each dreamer is named *She*.

At times, the dreamers imagine multiple versions of themselves— who they might be if they were French, for instance, or lived in France.

Sometimes they dream of their mothers or grandmothers, or other women they've known well, or women they wish they'd known better.

The women they dream about also dream and remember and imagine, maybe dreaming versions of *themselves*, younger or older.

Various images appear, first in one woman's dream, and then in another's.

These reoccurring images seem to twine in and out between the dreams, pleaching both the dreamers and the dreams.

One might be tempted to match the dreamer to the dream, or one might simply dream along with the women who dream.

SHE

A woman who remembers a trip to the south of France, and a moment when she wished her blonde hair were as dark as Cleopatra's.

A woman who is a photographer and a poet—"Why choose when you can be both?"

A woman who writes the word "elemental" in red lipstick on a paper napkin.

A woman who thinks she might have been a nun if she'd been born in the seventeenth century.

A woman whose French father read her legends and myths and French folktales when she was a child growing up in the Napa Valley.

A woman who can imagine falling in love again, perhaps with a Frenchman, perhaps with a man who lives in Provence.

A woman who sometimes dreams she is giving birth to an orchid.

A woman who once believed that a garden could heal anything.

A woman who married her Parisian lover a month after she graduated from Le Cordon Bleu Culinary School.

A woman who inherited a book about Redouté's paintings from her grandmother.

A woman who cut her hair very short after her husband died.

A woman who thinks her recurring daydreams about France might have started when she was a child, working on a puzzle.

A woman who once confided to a friend, "In French gardens, the statues of Greek gods and goddesses make me feel as if I'm not alone."

A woman who once dreamt of a town where the trees were made of bread.

A woman who teaches Religious Studies and is on sabbatical in France.

A woman who once wrote in her journal, "My life is like a piece of fabric, half of it dyed in story, half of it dyed in dream."

A woman whose interior design clients say things to her like, "I wish I could put together my life the way you put together a room."

A woman who writes for *Vogue* magazine, and extended her last trip to France so that she could volunteer at a refugee camp in Calais.

A woman who sometimes dreams about oracles and sometimes dreams about vagabonds.

A woman who thinks she will plant an orchard one day, and imagines entwined branches, weighted with pears.

A woman who once saw a folding screen with part of a woman's face painted on each panel and was surprised that the final panel revealed—not the entire face assembled, as she had anticipated—but an empty blue sky.

I

In the dream, the French Ambassador asks, "What do American women dream of when they dream about France?"

BEST USE

This room is the shade of yellow she always imagines, the shade that has more to do with light than color. The handmade pillows are mounded like waves across a four-poster bed.

The pillows, intricate cutwork and lace, were made long ago by a great-aunt who spent hours working beside an open window with a view of the sea. She had destined them for a room like this, in a town like this, far enough from Paris so a family with many children could have all the room they would need. With this in mind, she imagined her delicate pillows put to their best use on Sunday mornings, seized by the children of the house, who descend on their parents with great unity of purpose, pillows in hand, until their parents can no longer defend themselves and collapse across the sprawling bed with the full weight of their flailing children upon them.

In the great-aunt's imagination, this is a happy moment. The children are elated as they dream of triumphs to come. The parents are happy too; with the full weight of their children upon them, and the firmness of the bed beneath them, they pull the delicate pillows closer and dream of coffee cups filled with the sea.

HIP POCKET

Paris. A woman leans closer to the balcony window, holding back the voluminous white curtain. Its linen is nubby between her fingers.

The lower half of the balcony has a wrought iron railing, a *fleur-de-lis* pattern. The woman standing here knows that, from the street looking up, this wrought iron is attractive. But today, she is on the inside looking out, and she sees it as a barrier.

She knows this will be the last time she watches him walk away, that this final glimpse of him—the dip, the swing of his gait, the hand that burrows into his hip pocket, already checking for the key, although the car is blocks away—will become a fragment of a memory that returns to her, persistently.

But what happens if she lets the curtain drop and turns her back to the window? Then the memory that reappears will be of a woman, alone in a room, her back to a window, tugging the two sides of her cardigan closer together.

The woman who dreams of France wants to reach across time and space and touch this woman's shoulder. She wants the warmth of her hand to enter the Frenchwoman's memory. She wants to say, "Yes, the fragment will follow you. Persistently at first, then later perhaps only hauntingly, and, after many years, perhaps only lyrically."

BLEATING GOAT

The Frenchwoman she imagines has entered a renowned antique restorer's atelier near the Rue Saint Bernard, wondering if her broken Louis XVI dining chair can be mended.

The furniture restorer runs his hand along the chair's circular back, which is split apart at the apex. He laughs, "You bring me a severed moon and want it made whole again."

The Frenchwoman nods, "It was my grandmother's. My father wants to shuttle it off to the attic, but I don't."

The furniture restorer bends down a little, touches the severed chair back with his fingertips, and suddenly sees a goat in a field, head down, ready to butt.

"Did your grandmother keep goats?" he asks. "Your father didn't like them much."

"No, he didn't," she answers, too surprised not to respond.

"You have a bit of the goat in you, I think. Perhaps like your grandmother." He turns the chair a little, examining it from a slightly different angle. "You know it's been mended before?"

"Of course it has. My brother and I used it to get a goat out of a plum tree. I stood on the chair while my brother steadied it. The goat leapt into my arms and we all ended up in a heap on the ground with the broken chair at the bottom."

"Lucky you didn't break anything but the chair," he continues as he runs his hands over the splintered edges.

"Oh, we did," she answers. "My brother broke his wrist. So there we were, the bleating goat, my brother howling, my father racing from the house shouting, and then a sprint to the hospital."

"It can be done. Your whole moon."

As he writes up the estimate she looks around the workroom. There's a hand-painted sign, rainbow letters above the arched doorway leading to the storeroom. It says *Rempailleur de Rêve.* "Nice sign," she says. "From a happy customer?"

"My son made it for me when he was ten." He hands her the estimate. "Perhaps the next time you visit your father, take him chocolates—just a small box—maybe four pieces—but a kind he really likes, from a nice shop, tied with a ribbon. Tell him, 'If there were no goats and no unruly children, there would be no furniture restorers.'"

BURROWS BENEATH HER NAILS

One hundred and five. The Frenchwoman, she imagines, has been planting tulips all morning. Dirt burrows beneath her nails. One after another, the pudgy bulbs fill the palm of her hand. Roots dangle through her outstretched fingers as she rocks the bulbs back and forth, untangling the hairy rootlets; suspended mid-air, roots and rootlets seem to search for the soil below.

Her face is moist. The sun creeps past the mid-heaven. Her knees ache. She continues planting, a little bit in love with each bulb, releasing each one with that much reluctance, until she places the last bulb in its newly dug hole. It fits like an eye into a socket. She thinks, *Bulb, storehouse of tulip memory, seek what you can, seek what you must,* as she tamps the soil down over it.

The green knee cushion makes an adequate pillow. A little lie-down beside the newly planted bed, her hands on her belly, her elbows on the grass. To one side, the oak branches explore the sky. As her gaze rifles through the intersecting branches, she sees herself walking through a primeval forest, in Cathar Country, near Villar-en-Val.

Layers and layers of birdsong welcome her. She touches the underside of a fern where the spores hide. A "no path" sort of path, a whisper of a thing, leads her downhill, to the left, to the right, to the left, to the right, through shadows, through intermittent pools of bronzed light.

She descends until the path ends at a thatched enclosure. One step and she is over the threshold. Above her head, leaf-heavy branches mesh. Flowers, like new stars, sprout from the moss-soft earth.

The Frenchwoman sleeps within this shelter and dreams of a bird swooping down, tearing a rabbit to pieces, feasting, flying off with bits of flesh and fur and blood stuck to its body.

OLEANDER

In her dreams of a French churchyard, she sees pink flowers blooming on oleander bushes. In California, the place where she lives, oleanders are planted along freeways, between roads going north and south, east and west. They are considered good, low-maintenance, drought-tolerant shrubs—plants that can take care of themselves.

But in the Parisian churchyard she dreams of, beside white-carved columns, the oleanders deliver a different message. They say, "All you have rushed past must be fully seen. Nothing just takes care of itself."

SEARCHING TENDRILS AND SUCTION PADS

A woman is wearing translucent white linen. She appears at the upstairs window of her Provencal villa. She is looking down at the tubular trellis and at the white gravel path that runs perpendicular to the back of the villa. Clematis starts are planted in intervals beside the trellis frame. At this moment, she is thinking about tendrils and the suction pads on the underside of new leaves, the ingenuity of growth.

The arbor's empty trellis pleases her. Once, she cut her hair short, like Juliette Binoche in *Chocolat*, and the curves in her face, the double arc of her lips, the half-moon of her chin, the aerial arches of her eyebrows, all became more obvious, and she understood the harmony of her own features for the first time.

When she decided to restore this villa, she told the architect and landscape designer, "Let's use the arch as a recurring motif." She can see it now in the villa's arched windows and doors. She can also see it in the two curved benches facing each other, one on either side of the lobelia circle surrounding the sundial. And, of course, she can see the motif repeated again and again in the arc of the trellis, atop each pair of uprights as they file two-by-two away from the house across the lawn.

Because it is so new, the garden could seem stark. But she imagines it as it will one day be, when the trellis has disappeared beneath the rampant, saucer-sized clematis, and the arches that support the vines are no longer visible.

She hears the crunch of footsteps on new gravel. The timer on her desk chimes. The mille-feuille. She turns from the window. She can almost taste the pastry cream.

WHISKING EGG WHITES

A woman in Paris is busy at her kitchen counter, whisking egg whites for a soufflé. Two tablespoons of lemon zest and the juice from one tangerine stand ready in saucers. As she brings the whisk down and around, she remembers herself as a child, perched on a stool beside the kitchen table, watching her mother do this.

The woman in Paris imagines a young woman in San Francisco about her daughter's age, in a farmers' market, with a string shopping bag over one shoulder, the sort of young woman who bought a whisk with her first paycheck.

She whispers in this young woman's ear, "The tangerines would make a lovely soufflé. You'll need a lemon too, for zest. Then keep it simple, a roasted chicken with potatoes and a bit of Swiss chard sautéed in vermouth. A cheese course, chèvre, Camembert— whatever you like. Then the big finish—the soufflé served with chunks of chocolate-covered hazelnuts, very dark chocolate. It will take their breath away."

The woman in San Francisco doesn't actually hear the Frenchwoman's voice, but she moves through the farmers' market, gathering lemons, tangerines, and Swiss chard, as if someone is guiding her hand.

CACTUS BOTTLE

It is Sunday morning in a village with one shopping street—a bar, a café, and an antique shop facing the sea. Sunlight is having a field day, skimming along the vintage perfume bottles lined up on a table in front of the antique shop. The light releases a flock of colors: emerald, teal, ruby, tangerine.

She spies what she wants in the last row at the back of the table, but doesn't touch it. Instead, she picks up a St. Louis beauty near the front, cobalt blue with a white serpent etched around the base. It reminds her somehow of Cleopatra. She asks the proprietress, *"Combien?"* When she hears the price, she shakes her head, *"Trop cher."*

She touches several other bottles, admiring the stoppers. Every one of them its own melody of faceted glass: the swan with such good posture; twin water nymphs, one combing the other's hair; a hummingbird perched on a cut glass globe.

She holds one more bottle up to the light—amber, hand-blown with a teardrop stopper, probably Czechoslovakian—then she puts it down and turns as if to walk away. But at the last moment, she glances at the table again and pretends to be surprised. "Oh, look what's hiding in the last row. Not very feminine." In fact, the Lalique cactus bottle she's been coveting, a sphere covered with black-tipped white spikes, looks as if it were designed by an alien from outer space.

As she picks it up to check for a signature, she wonders who owned it before. She pauses momentarily and looks out at the sea as the image of an American jazz musician slowly forms in her mind. Judging from his narrow lapels and tie, it must be the 1950s. He is in France because the French are crazy for jazz and because being black doesn't mean the same thing here as it means in America. She sees him lift the bottle, surprised by its heft. Leaded glass.

It feels like a baseball in his hand and reminds him of his childhood passion, a good pitch, the arm extending, the release, the ball flying through space, going somewhere, untethered, like a perfectly played note.

The signature is there, *Lalique*. Of course she'll buy it, just as the American trumpeter would have bought it, perhaps for himself, perhaps for a woman he loved.

SEARCHING THE SIDEWALK AND STREET BELOW

Somewhere in Paris there is an apartment building with a wrought iron *escalier en colimaçon*, spiraling up. As this apartment building's elegant inhabitants aged, they installed an elevator matching the design of the original stairway.

A Frenchwoman in her forties lives on the sixth floor of the building. For the sake of her thighs and calves, she uses the stairs, not the elevator. But she likes the elevator for her guests, so that they don't arrive on her doorstep winded or flushed.

Everything in the apartment has been chosen with care. The Baccarat vase, filled with overblown roses, sits on a Prouvé coffee table, just off center, in front of an Adnet daybed, black leather with two husky bolsters, one at each end.

She wears her hair in a blunt cut, but usually it is pulled back, away from her face. Her red lipstick has a violet undertone that matches the roses. Most of the clothes she wears are black, but she is always pleased when gray or navy swirl back into style.

Today, she stands at the double-hung window, searching the sidewalk and street below, one shoulder engulfed in the georgette drapery. The table has been laid. The champagne chilled. Her favorite moment is always this one. It is this moment, brimming with anticipation, just before her guests arrive, that she loves.

RANGEFINDER

She wonders what it would have been like to be a student in France when she was in her twenties. She envisions herself at a sidewalk café in Paris, wearing tight Levi's, her long hair curling between her shoulder blades, her father's old Leica Rangefinder camera in her lap. She'd be sipping coffee, making it last, as she penned a journal entry in her Moleskine notebook.

She'd look up from time to time at the groups of people chatting at nearby tables, and long for a quiet place like the Cathedral at Lourdes. As she sipped her coffee, savoring its warmth, she'd see herself in the doorway at the back of the church, watching an elderly woman, a pilgrim kneeling in prayer. She'd wait patiently with her Leica until this pilgrim stepped forward into the light.

NAPKIN

She would like to avoid anything too stylized. She does not want to see the reflection of a potted orchid on the glass surface of a framed photograph, which has been placed intentionally to capture the orchid's reflection, so the photograph itself is viewed through the orchid's semitransparent reflection.

Instead, she wants a breeze to suddenly lift a young woman's hair. She wants the same breeze to toss a crumpled napkin off an abandoned café table, sending it bouncing across the square. She wants a dog with drooping ears to take off barking after the napkin. She wants the young woman to look up from her notebook and laugh, laugh because she is surprised by the sudden envy she feels for the dog.

SUN

She sees herself on a crowded street corner in Paris, waiting for the light to change. The man in front of her is tall. She stares at the back of his coat, wondering if she is headed in the right direction.

When the green light appears, the pedestrians crowded around her press forward. The man in the coat strides off the curb into the crosswalk. Now she sees it, the iconic wall of windows in the distance, her destination on the bank of the Seine: the Institut du Monde Arabe, designed by Jean Nouvel and constructed in 1981.

Nouvel said that these windows were inspired by the *mashrabiya* and the camera, a twelfth-century invention melded to a nineteenth-century invention. Both, she thinks, designed by people who knew how to put their ears to the sun.

KNOW IT IS A FOX

When the iridescent blue wing of the dragonfly appears at the open window, beside the white rose with dots like blood on its inner petals, the woman who daydreams about France thinks perhaps it isn't necessary to see the view from this window, the vase holding the rose, or the interior of the Frenchwoman's kitchen.

But then she wonders. *What made the Frenchwoman choose this rose and not another? When its wedding-night petals opened, did the pinpricks of red surprise her, or had she foreseen them as a soothsayer might?*

She wants a pot of steeping coffee to appear on the counter beneath the open window, so its aroma draws the Frenchwoman back to the kitchen. She wants to see this woman's fingers, twisted as century-old bittersweet vines, touch the vase into existence.

Then she wants the old woman to hear a sudden cry, know it is a fox, and look up, out the window, beyond the dragonfly's iridescent blue wing. Then perhaps hay bales will appear like megalithic remnants rolled and dropped at random intervals across the unsuspecting field.

RABBIT-FUR BAG

A Frenchwoman, with straight white hair falling to the small of her back, sits at a card table pulling puzzle pieces one by one from a rabbit-fur bag. Before she places each piece in the puzzle, she holds it in the palm of one hand and folds her fingers over it, feeling its contours, its dips and bulges.

Through the open window, the terra-cotta rooftops of Collioure can be seen sloping down to the Mediterranean. She looks out the window and imagines waves covered with puzzle pieces. Poseidon, Thetis, Eurogome.

INHABITED

In adolescence, she would have wanted to flee from the image of this village, this hill town in Provence, where all of the homes are made of the same stone as the hill itself, where the abandoned dwellings exist side by side with those that are inhabited. Not long ago, when she first encountered this village in a daydream, it was hard to distinguish the town from the hill, the inhabited dwellings from the abandoned.

Now, she wonders what it would have been like to grow up in a stone town, to walk past ruins on the way to school. What would all of that past in the present do? Perhaps it would make individual destinies seem like absurd variations on already-too-often-stated themes, or perhaps it would bring out the flavor of life, intensifying both the bitter and the sweet. She isn't sure. But today she longs for the richness, the hauntedness of a life among these stones. She thinks that perhaps the depth of village life, knowing every face you see, could be comforting.

When this village lingers in her thoughts today, she sees bits of an old path that must connect the lower part of the village to the older part on the hilltop above. Though the entire path is not visible, she is certain that, if she were actually in this town with her feet on this path, the way would become clear.

CORNUCOPIA

In the foreground, she imagines a vineyard, rows of grapevines trailing down a gradual slope; beyond the vineyard, a stand of cork oak trees and, even farther, beyond the trees, deep in the valley at the base of the hills, a half-timbered, thatched cottage with a row of iris growing along the roof's ridgeline. Daffodils and jonquils fill stone troughs, one on either side of the open front door.

Inside the house, benches flank a hand-hewn table. Part of a meal has been set out. There are several crusty round loaves, and a bowl carved like a cornucopia is overflowing with green apples.

A young woman enters this room, sits down at the table, and places a bowl of cracked walnuts beside the apples. Then the characters from all of the folktales that have ever been told come in to join her. As they enter through the open door, each contributes to the feast: platters laden with roasted beef, bottles of red wine, hunks of gruyere, gouda, and Cheshire. Dates in baskets woven from the reeds of the Nile. A cask of Mongolian soup with dumplings.

These characters have journeyed to this table from all of the corners of the world, from all of the corners of time. They eat and drink and laugh and, after the meal is finished, each one takes a turn telling a tale that she or he alone knows. As one speaks, the others listen. Words fill the room. One weaves a tale about a broken bowl found beside a well. One weaves a tale of a garnet ring hidden within a chimney. Those who listen see each detail clearly.

In the background, swallows fly in and out through the open door.

DECIDES TO PLUCK HER EYEBROWS

She decides to pluck her eyebrows. Magnifying mirror in hand, she is after a look that seems Parisian, arched. She works slowly, thinking of Audrey Hepburn in *Sabrina*, a black-and-white film she watched repeatedly as a teenager on a portable TV, after school, in her upstairs bedroom with the volume low.

Sabrina, the awkward but tenderhearted, daydreaming chauffer's daughter, who returns to America from culinary school in Paris transformed into a young woman of the world, still tenderhearted but now wearing Givenchy, a black double-breasted traveling suit. Sabrina's face and arrestingly styled eyebrows are framed by a white turban, also designed by Givenchy.

Today, she wants an updated version of those Sabrina brows, dramatic, but with a softer outline, more natural looking. As she shapes her brows, she imagines a bathroom in Paris where an antique mirror hangs on a wall above a pedestal sink. When she looks closer, she notices that the floor in the bathroom in Paris is exactly the same unpolished limestone as the floor in her own bathroom, the floor she is actually standing on.

ALMOST BURIED

She sees herself wearing a forties swingback jacket as she wanders through the Sunday morning flea market in Lille, along Jean-Baptiste Lebas Boulevard. The sun is coming up as she rifles through boxes of old records, used books, and magazines.

List? Of course she has one: vintage Givenchy jacket; Cartier watch from the twenties or thirties; Braquenié or Boussac fabric remnants; *Elle* magazines from the fifties or sixties, especially the November 1962 issue with candid shots of Jeanne Moreau.

A list provides focus. Essential. But she also knows how to let her eyes rove until they find something unexpected and intriguing, like the corner of white paper she notices near the bottom of a cardboard box, almost buried under records from the 1950s.

She pulls at the paper, shimmies it out from under the records, and finds herself holding *Orphée*, the shooting script, signed on the inside cover by both Cocteau and Jean Marais. She drops the script back into the cardboard box. "What would you like for this box of old records?" she asks.

GRINDING LAPIS LAZULI

Today, she imagines herself walking out of the eighth arrondissement, past women with precisely groomed brows, wearing this season's Chanel and Dior. She walks past a boutique window filled with Darel handbags and mannequins posed as if they'd invented style.

She walks and walks until she finds a bench not too far from the bookstalls, where she sits facing the Seine. Her half-closed eyes skim the water's surface as she dreams of Anastasia, the fifteenth-century miniaturist who lived near this spot and honed her talent by illustrating manuscripts in a windowless room, laying down gold leaf borders, grinding lapis lazuli that had come all the way from Afghanistan.

BETWEEN DESTINATIONS

She dreams of a cloister in France inhabited by a nun who exists outside of time, in a series of perpetual gestures, stepping from darkness into light, from heat into shade. This woman in her black habit does not think about being inside or out as she enters the cloisters—she is simply alone for a moment between destinations. A small book is tucked in her hand, the tip of one finger curled in to hold her place.

In a moment, this nun will reach the shady side of the cloisters, sit on a bench, and read aloud softly. As she speaks, the words of this passage will annihilate everything: the fragrance of the lavender in the stone planter beside her, and the sound of water in the fountain behind her. She does not anticipate any of this; instead, she listens intently and hears the hem of her skirt brushing the stones she walks upon. She hears this sound first as an extension of her own heartbeat, and then farther away from her body, as the pulse of this place.

NAVIGATION

She imagines French explorers dragging their loaded sleds across Antarctica. One explorer wrote that his greatest fear about the expedition was not the impossible cold or the complex navigation. He was most afraid, he said, that after all of the preparation and planning, they would arrive in Antarctica and simply not be able to drag the sleds with their four-hundred-pound loads.

When she reads this, it makes her think about certain moments in her own life, those moments when she defies what she feels are the limits of her own body, the limits of her own expectations, the moments when she is no longer the dreamer dreaming, when she is someone else, actually inhabiting the place she dreams of, a mountain in the Pyrenees, or a hill town in Provence.

She thinks of these moments as gifts, the repetition of these gifts as blessings. She is not certain what makes these moments possible. Perhaps it is her willingness to haunt these landscapes and be haunted by them.

When she thinks of the polar explorers, she admires their courage. She admires their ghostly presence in the endless white landscape. Willingly, gladly, she makes herself ghostly in order to enter the place she dreams of.

II

In the dream, an upturned umbrella catches the rain.

CAUGHT IN A CORRIDOR

The Frenchwoman she dreams of returns to Lyon, to the house where she grew up. It is Sunday, nearly midday, and soon the entire family will assemble for lunch. But at the moment, the woman she dreams of is caught in a corridor that connects two sides of the house. The ceiling seems too low, the walls too close.

The woman she dreams of does not go forward into the kitchen, where she knows her mother is about to lift a perfectly cooked roast from the oven and present it to the assembled family. Instead, distracted, the woman turns, wanders out onto the terrace. She wants a breath of fresh air, not this tightness she feels in her chest. But this is the garden of the house she grew up in, filled with its own contradictions.

She moves away from the terrace, where the wrought iron table is already set for a four-course lunch. She moves past the oversized bench, half-filled with potted succulents and cymbidiums. She is drawn to the deeper greens beneath an oak at the far end of the garden. Under its crisscrossing branches, within the dappled light, with the bark beneath her hands, she is suddenly moved by the tree's success. Its branches reach far beyond her childhood expectations.

One day, she will be able to articulate the impulse that has driven her out of the house and across the lawn. It will be something about artifice and alienation, about excessive embellishment obscuring beauty. But today, she only knows that the table and chairs look like a cluster of over-polished teeth: too white, too ornate, a false smile in the midday sun.

HANDS MOVE INDEPENDENTLY

The French herb jars gleam. They are porcelain, antique. One is missing its lid, but the rest seem well preserved.

These herb jars are numbered, not named. The larger the jar, the lower the number.

She can't imagine living with this nameless system, where she would have to remember which number corresponded to which herb. The sense of order required for remembering the contents of these antique jars has nothing to do with the distractions of her daily life. Her mind is so often caught up in lists of things to do, or in daydreams of France, that her hands move independently while her thoughts are elsewhere.

A KNIGHT AND LADY EMERGE

The empty crate, the tapestry beside it rolled out across the stone floor. She takes a preparatory breath, then exhales and lets her eyes range top to bottom, left to right, the corners, the whole. Medieval. French, not Flemish. Created perhaps fifty years after the famous unicorn tapestry.

Mille fleurs, a thousand flowers, cover the background. Out of the flowers, a knight and lady emerge. A bird rests on the lady's shoulder. A fox stands at attention. The knight watches a deer escaping into the trees. The deer's nose glows in the greenery, a bit of moon fallen to earth. She remembers part of the explanation for this glow, something about blue threads layered over black. It must be a very deep blue.

She circles the room, turning on a few lights. Sixteenth- and seventeenth-century furniture line the room's perimeter. Paintings hang on the walls, salon style. The Louis XIV table she uses for a desk is near the door.

This tapestry won't go to the highest bidder, the American tech entrepreneur, or the Swiss cable mogul. Other treasures for them, but not this. This tapestry will go to an elderly viscount who has, with the utmost patience and the utmost perseverance, been restoring a family chateau in the Loire, piece by piece, for decades.

Once each year, he invites her to lunch. Shows her his progress, a recent find or simply the way a newly restored corner of the garden is coming back to life. The first year she visited him, they laughed as if he spoke metaphorically when he said, "The chateau tells me what it yearns for, whispers in my ear at dusk."

She will spend some time researching the tapestry. Once she knows the name of each flower, and its symbolism, once she finds out how the weavers created that glow, she'll call the viscount.

MOSS

She dreams of a series of stone arches. From a distance, each arch seems to frame a small portion of the garden, functioning the way a picture frame might, helping her focus on the details within the frame. As she approaches each arch, the sense of framing intensifies; she sees more details: the jigsaw curve of a mulberry branch; a palm frond dipping back to earth. But when she arrives beneath an arch, and stands within its mossy shadow looking out, she realizes that the arches have also been placed to reveal each of the garden's most striking views.

One arch frames a keyhole topiary through which she sees Poseidon's bronze back glisten as he rises from a fountain. Another arch leads her eyes to an arbor heavy with Peace roses, like the ones Steichen photographed in Voulangis, 1914. They say it was his last photo in France before the Great War. Standing under another arch, she sees an *allée* of cypress bordering a gravel path. The trees seem to continue without end.

She follows the path from arch to arch, as if an old friend is giving her an intimate tour of his beloved garden, a friend who knows exactly the right moment to be silent so she can see.

SPINNING NIB

Seated at a desk beside an open window, her fingers search for the pen she eventually finds beneath scattered papers. She rolls it back and forth between her palms, thinks about its gold nib spinning, thinks about the patch of green beyond the dormer window where bearded iris are about to open.

She feels herself opening too, remembers the pleasures of other days like this, one day in particular, long ago. She remembers falling asleep in Chateau de la Roche Courbon's famous garden, the chateau that Pierre Loti called "sleeping beauty of the forest."

She sees herself lying on her back in the sun-steeped grass, her handbag-sized backpack tucked under her head, her arms flung out at her sides. Her eyelids close because they cannot stay open, because the air skimming her bare arms is more comforting than a caress.

BOUGAINVILLEA

Spring in Marseilles. A third-story apartment, the wall outside the bedroom window is covered with bougainvillea. A young woman rearranges her bedroom furniture, placing the bed beneath the window so she can pick bougainvillea without getting out of bed.

Whatever age she is, she will remember this version of herself: naked, embroidered sheets, their well-worn linen skimming over her breasts, her legs forming a diamond as she sits on the bed, the soles of her feet touching, the space between her legs gradually filling with bougainvillea.

As she plucks the wing-like bracts, she remembers a childhood longing, the desire to *be* the garden. The drooping tulip. The rose in bud. The flaming zinnia. The cotton-candy dianthus. The desire to be the pink, the blue, the pale peach, the green, the ground cover with its star-shaped flowers. To be the cypress rising high around the perimeter, whispering, *This is where the garden ends.*

That desire she felt long before she knew ashes could be scattered like stars beneath such trees.

BEYOND THE SEA

She sees herself on a grassy terrace, above a vineyard, a new bride. She and her newly minted husband, the groom, are about to circle the dance floor. Their loved ones gather around them, forming an irregular circle. As they wait for the music to begin, her family chats softly in English, his family chats just as softly in French. Their voices intermingle, then become hushed when they hear the first few notes of "Beyond the Sea."

She looks into her husband's eyes, then lifts her train. Her arm rests comfortably on his shoulder. Their foreheads touch, not just for a moment, but until the song ends.

Later in the evening, when they pause between dances, a waiter appears at their side, handing each of them a glass of champagne. As she looks into her glass, she sees bubbles clustering around the rim, jostling, nuzzling.

She takes her husband's hand. "Just look at these champagne bubbles. When I was younger, my daydreams about France arrived, bubbling and jostling and nuzzling behind my eyes until they rose up, like little bubbles of light passing my forehead. Up and up. Bubbling right through the top of my skull, as this champagne soon will."

She holds her glass up to his lips. He takes a sip, kisses her forehead, then draws her closer as he kisses the nape of her neck.

VOICE

She daydreams about a stairway, curling up the outside of a building. The railing is wrought iron, robin's egg blue, not black. It goes up and up, through a series of stone arches, one for each flight. The stairs lead to a rooftop garden where iceberg roses and dwarf lemon trees bloom in terra-cotta pots. Deep white cushions cover the garden furniture, which is also wrought iron, painted light blue like the railing below.

In the evenings, the French couple sits here sipping cognac mixed with raspberry juice, over ice, in glasses rimmed with a twist of orange, and the woman tells the man a story as the sun sets over the Marais. The subject of the story isn't important; it could be about anything, something she read in the paper, a childhood memory recalled, or a bit of conversation she overheard while walking down the street. The cognac isn't really important either. It is the sound of her voice in the disappearing light that he loves.

AS SUDDENLY AS HE ENTERED

The house in Arles marks the conclusion of a tree-lined drive. She thinks of these trees as sycamores, but she knows some people call them plane trees or buttonwoods. Their tall, arching branches create a canopy above the drive. Framed within this canopy, part of the house becomes visible, one white wall and the front door, painted the green of the sycamore leaves.

She remembers sitting at her kitchen table, coffee cup in hand, a sewing box still open beside her. The cotton blouse she has mended rests in her lap. It belongs to her daughter, who is asleep in an upstairs bedroom, eyes closed, honey-blonde hair cascading across the pillow.

The button came off last night when her daughter was washing dishes after dinner. Her daughter was telling her about the new man in her life, the man who is too old for her, who has ex-wives, grown children, and too much wealth. She wants this man to leave her daughter's life as suddenly as he entered it.

She puts down the coffee cup and slowly rewinds the gray thread, thread she'd already had in the sewing box because it matches the curtains on her daughter's bedroom windows, matches the bark of the sycamores that line the drive. She returns the sewing box to the shelf and walks out under these trees. Tones in the shades of her own honey-blonde hair are scattered in the wild grasses surrounding the trees. As she moves beneath the intersecting branches, she looks up at the sun-drenched canopy, feels at home within the colors she loves.

If she could enter her daughter's dreams, she knows what image she would place there—an image she would call *first love*. She sees it clearly: a room like an open field in Provence, but with one of these trees at each corner, and the floor a meadow rising out of the dark moist earth. In the center of this room, a marriage bed of woven grapevines covered with woodbine, the species of honeysuckle known for its fragrance, its mauve and pale yellow flowers. The species her daughter chose and planted long ago beneath her bedroom window.

If she prayed, she would pray now, but instead she finds herself in a deep state of longing. Aloud she says, "Let a young man my daughter's own age enter her life. Let them be drawn together by fragrance, a familiar scent at the base of the neck. Let their life together be a drawing down through the pale yellow into the deep mauve center."

PALM THRUST UP

One day, there are red poppies in the olive grove, and she thinks it must be springtime in the place she dreams of. Bits and pieces of this grove have inhabited her imagination for years, showing up in the empty spaces between thoughts, like photographs from a trip not yet taken.

She loves this grove in Provence, these well-tended, low-growing, evenly spaced trees; their gray-and-black bark; the way the branches open, spreading out like the fingers of a generous hand, palm thrust up toward the sun. She has seen this grove from a hundred angles, always in snapshots, and today, when it appears in its entirety, row upon row, moving across the gentle hills, she is only surprised by the poppies: *Eleusis*, she thinks, *the ancient flowers among the ancient trees.*

FOLDED ALONG THE DOTTED LINES

About an hour left up here in the attic before the sun peaks, bakes. She sits cross-legged in a summer skirt, rifling through cardboard boxes, sorting ephemera as nostalgic as faded chintz. The things her grandmother saved.

She places what she'll keep in an upturned box lid: a photo of Fontevraud Abbey looking like an oversized castle; her grandmother's handwriting on the back, "Monsieur Disney, you got it wrong. Your films conjured puny castles far too small for us."

On top of the photo she adds a yellowed envelope that she is surprised to find, marked "1949, Eleanor of Aquitaine paper dolls." Inside, cut as close to the line as possible with elementary school precision by her grandmother's eight-year-old hand, the queen's crown, veil, and drop-waist gown. All the white tabs cut out too, then folded along the dotted lines. The paper doll's figure is remarkably like Katharine Hepburn's, who played Eleanor in the 1968 film *The Lion in Winter*.

Eleanor, who carried the crown of two kingdoms, bore ten children, outlived eight of them and both of her husbands. Survived sixteen years under house arrest then rose again, ruled again, with her son Richard the Lionheart.

She opens another envelope. This one labeled "2007." The year after the surgeons took her grandmother's second breast.

Inside the envelope there's a photo, one her grandmother took. The photo captures the light as it descends from Fontevraud's upper reaches and lands on Eleanor's gisant, a white slash across her plaster cheek.

BUNDLE

South of the Loire, a woman makes hand-dipped beeswax tapers in the cave her late husband once used for aging goat cheese. She had not made candles since she was a child helping her grandmother with the dipping and the trimming of wicks, but one night after her husband's death, she dreamt of the empty cave and sensed her grandmother's presence there.

Now, each time she gazes at the melting wax, the heat from the cauldron rises, warming her face. And as the muscles beneath her eyes relax, she imagines herself feather-covered, rolling the almost perfect sphere of an owl's white egg between her palms, thinking of the mountain, craggy as an old man's face, and of her own goat-like self, climbing with bundles of wax and wick and kindling.

When the sparks ignite beneath the cauldron, they seem to release all her husband's good intentions. A lifetime of them, those he managed to fulfill and those he only dreamed of. They circle her, plume, permeate the mountain's scooped out interior and the honey-tipped bees singing in her fingers.

DISAPPEARED INTO

This winding path, the woodland cradling it—a place she inhabits, a place that inhabits her—time and again she has followed this path to the cave's entrance, disappeared into the bowl-shaped interior, and rested against the rough, unpainted walls.

This place, completely of the earth, has hovered in her imagination since childhood. Sometimes she wonders if it is in Arkansas, with other caves nearby, or someplace more wild— Idaho, Wyoming, or Montana. Existing only in her imagination, without a larger context, has never diminished the capacity of the cave to offer her solace.

Then one day, while leafing through a *National Geographic* magazine at the dentist's office, she notices a photograph of a woodland path, the cave's entrance so familiar, so much like the place she dreams of. As she lifts the magazine closer, the caption comes into focus. She reads, "Early man, Neolithic site, Les Eyzies, France." *Of course, of course,* she thinks, *the cave is not in Arkansas, or Idaho, or Montana, but in France, the place I so often dream of.*

FOLLOWING

October in the south of France. She sees herself following the sheep as the shepherds do. Her days spent walking over grassy Provençal slopes. Her nights spent sleeping outside beneath distinct stars. When it rains, there will be days filled with wet walking, and nights like the inside of a boiled wool overcoat, starless.

She imagines evenings spent listening to the shepherds tell stories as they sit around the campfire together. The sheep would always be nearby, their clustered shadows in the knee-high grass, their collective breathing, voluminous, comforting.

MORE CLEARLY

Formed, unformed. Formed, unformed. Images arrive, linger, depart; sharp clear images followed by patterns of light and dark. A rose opens until one white petal fills the entire frame. This rose is followed by muffled voices and the sound of feet shuffling.

Then something in the shadows that she wants to see more clearly. Then something further away, partially obscured by a wall or tree—who could say at such a distance? Then no background, no foreground, just a sense of space, an empty, white pause.

Then the whiteness gathers into itself, stretches, becomes a ball. Hands reach into the frame. She sees a green marble slab underneath as the dough is lifted, turned, and sprinkled with flour. She watches—not sure what shape this dough will take— baguette, bâtard, brioche?

Formed, unformed. Formed, unformed. The rhythm of her imagination.

RECLINING ON A DIVAN

She imagines a woman in Paris, heiress to a steel empire, posed before a three-paneled mirror in a designer's atelier, alternately viewing front, back, and sides. No smile. Just that lioness gaze.

It is 1956. The mannequins in this atelier have a stately presence, as if they were once vessels transporting sacred oil across the sea, as if they are demonstrating how to live. It's not how the heiress wants to live. She wants to laugh and dance, to drink Dom Pérignon in the back seat of a cabriole. What is the point of being an heiress if you can't do that?

She'll have this dress and the Van Cleef & Arpels evening bag she saw a few minutes ago, the silk clutch with the hand-cast gold clasp—a reclining woman with faceted sapphire eyes and ruby mouth. The moment she saw that clasp she thought, *That woman knows how to hunt, while for all the world making it look as if she's reclining on a divan.*

In a whirl of blue chiffon, the heiress turns from the mirror and, in that moment, remembers the man she saw an hour ago at Café Deux Magots. Mostly he kept reading his journal, making notes in the margins. But he caught her staring at him when he looked up.

She doesn't need to find out his name. If he's worth knowing, he'll be clever enough to find her.

NOT FAR FROM THE CHAMP DE MARS

A young American tourist with several shopping bags finds herself poking around a lingerie store. She hadn't really intended to come inside, but here she is, surrounded by peach silk, and rows and rows of bras on satin hangers.

She suspects that these bras possess secret properties, properties that are entirely French. What could they do for her, anyway? Could they lift her breasts to new heights? And what would her raised breasts look like—maybe a little too pert, artificial? Perhaps she could get used to it, in order to fulfill that other dream, of a long narrow ribcage leading to a gently tapered waist.

At last, she turns away from the bras. She decides to buy a camisole and leave the mystery of the French bra untouched, like the ancient caves near Les Eyzies that have been closed to the public, their paintings long preserved, protected from human breath.

BETWEEN HER FINGERS

The saleswomen in the fabric store on 7th Avenue in New York all move as if they are exhausted, as if they have been tied to the mast of their own insignificance and tongue-lashed with songs of lost love and broken hearts since they were teenagers in the 1960s. In these women's arms, the fabric looks waterlogged, as if the bolts are so heavy the women will be dragged to the shop's linoleum floor, where they will spend the rest of their lives lost in daydreams about nearly forgotten shipwrecks at the bottom of the sea.

She wonders what these saleswomen would think if they could see what she daydreams about, a *de tissus*, in Paris, where the French saleswomen glide like swans, their chins slightly tucked, backs straight, necks arched. The fabric bolts buoyant in their arms.

One of the French saleswomen in particular holds her attention. She wears a dress she must have designed herself—accordion pleats on the right near the hemline, a diagonal ruffle at the waist on the left; buttons navigate a single sleeve spiraling from elbow to wrist.

This woman cradles the fabric bolt in her arms as she approaches the cutting table. Half-turn by half-turn she unwinds it, letting the pattern reveal itself bit by bit, as it slides between her fingers along a stainless-steel yardstick.

OUT OF THE TUMBLED ROCKS

She wants to turn to her friend and say, "We've made it this far." But as they approach the summit they've been climbing toward all day, she doesn't have the breath.

Up ahead, two friends may already be resting at the pinnacle. Two more friends trail behind, their pace slower because they like to chat and photograph wildflowers along the path. She last saw them crouched beside a mini landslide where pink Rosaceae sprang out of the tumbled rocks.

The six women have known each other since college. They train all winter for these hikes. For ten days each summer, they hike a different section of the Pyrenees. So close to the Spanish border a layer of constraint peels away. Sunscreen and hats protect their faces, but for these ten days, they let their arms and legs brown.

Circles of white flesh beneath their watches will help them remember their own weary, loosened limbs, the open skies punched by raptors, and the trembling stars illuminating the owl's question.

GRAVES OF THE FAMOUS

Today she visits Père Lachaise Cemetery. A friend recently gave her a map with the graves of the famous already marked. She walks past the tribe mourning Jim Morrison, past the cluster of young women photographing themselves at Colette's grave, past the couple holding hands, earbuds tucked in, leaning against the cenotaph of Maria Callas.

She will only visit one grave. She will not take flowers. Instead, she will take a creek-rubbed stone, no bigger than her thumb. She looks forward to adding her stone to the cascade of stones left atop the headstone by those who have come to pay tribute before her. She sees this gesture, the hand releasing the stone, as a declaration to all those who pass by that the one buried here inhabits memory and imagination, exists for her, as alive as those who live.

THE LONG-HANDLED SPOON

It's late afternoon. An American tourist who has spent the morning hiking along the old road to Vézelay sits at an open-air café on the bank of the Cure River, navigating a sundae that reminds her of her childhood favorite, a towering ice cream concoction called The Matterhorn.

She nudges her long-handled spoon down through the sundae's layers; through the whipped cream laced with lavender, chopped hazelnuts, and sea salt; through the hot fudge sauce; through the vanilla ice cream, all the way down to the bottom of the bowl and the American fudge brownie she's been craving.

Because her table is by the water's edge, every now and then the breeze covers her with spray from the waterfall fifteen feet below. As she eats, she overhears a tour guide explaining local history to an elderly group of American tourists seated at a table beside her. She eats slowly, smiles, and listens for the rhythm of an accent like her own.

Then, gradually, their voices blend and ebb as she begins to imagine a different rhythm, a steady *tap, tap, tap*. In her mind's eye, she sees a blackened pot tied to the back of a pilgrim's wagon on the old road to Vézelay. The pot is tapping against the cast-iron kettle hanging beside it. The pilgrim sits on the wagon seat; his weight shifts side to side as the horse steps along. His foot finds the beat and he begins to tap his toes.

III

In the dream, the bouquet is so big,
two hands are needed to hold it.

THROUGHOUT THE WINTER

She imagines a nineteenth-century marble bathtub. Her mother would have described it as "deep enough to drown in." But she doesn't see it that way. She is simply dreaming of luxury, towers of bubbles and water up to her chin. She asks herself, now, having arrived in this tub, with a stack of Frette towels beside it, *What would I dream of next?* That's easy. She laughs.

The marble tub is in a chateau in the Dordogne, in a bathroom off an upstairs bedroom. French doors in the bedroom open onto a balcony, where the breakfast table has already been laid.

As she steps through the French doors, the air feels cool after her steamy bath. A familiar fragrance. She closes her eyes momentarily, letting her fingers play along the cuff of her charmeuse robe as she sifts through memories until she finds one of herself, at age eight, curled up on a porch swing at her grandmother's house, looking across the garden at a white fence covered with honeysuckle.

Someone must have planted honeysuckle beneath this balcony. Later, she will walk downstairs and look for it, but right now, she opens her eyes and looks out at the garden below. She imagines the greenhouse on the far side of the golden moon maples. It is not visible, but she has been told it is there.

Because of this greenhouse, she knows, there will be roses throughout the winter, and orchids, bright orchids like butterflies on arching stems.

A DIFFERENT STORY

Today she dreams of a grandmama with a face like a stewed apple, sitting on a Louis XIV chair, holding a skeleton key attached to a mammoth tassel. The grandmama has had this key so long that she can't remember what it unlocks, but the chair is a different story. She remembers the day she and her husband bought it, their first piece of real furniture.

After her husband died five years ago, the grandmama had the chair reupholstered in damask, brown, like his eyes. Damask, an old-fashioned fabric; her husband would have liked that.

IN THE MOUNTAINS OF PERSIA

She is dreaming about France the way she might dream of exploring a house she has never been inside. She stands in a circular entryway, looking up at a Baccarat chandelier. As she looks down and to the left, she sees double doors with brass handles. The doors open. She steps through them and finds herself drifting through a salon with high ceilings and a series of French doors at either end.

More crystal. Baccarat sconces. Sofas and chairs are clustered around low-slung tables. The furniture rests on carpets woven in the mountains of Persia hundreds of years before she was born. She walks toward a pedestal table, stands beside it, and touches the objects displayed: a lacquered box; an alabaster vase; a magnifying glass, its ram's-horn handle carved into a mermaid's tail.

Near the center of the room, an indigo sofa beckons. She steps toward it, sinks into its down cushions. The cushions are covered in jade-green cut velvet. She strokes their three-inch persimmon fringe. She begins to feel as if she could sit here forever, but then she sees a Pleyel grand piano across the room, in front of the French doors. Its keys remind her of black irises she once gathered into a bouquet, then placed in a white porcelain pitcher beside her kitchen sink.

She rises from the sofa and makes her way across the room. Briefly, she stands beside the piano, then sits down on its sun-warmed bench as she imagines the first strains of Arvo Pärt's "Mirror in the Mirror." Eyes closed, she is silent as the music plays. Silent after it ends.

Light between her lashes as her eyelids open. To her left, an arched doorway opens to a hallway painted a shade of lavender so pale it almost looks white. At the end of the hallway, Sonia Delaunay's 1907 painting, *Jeune Fille Endormie.*

Strands of loose hair graze her cheek, a breeze. One of the French doors is ajar. She steps toward it, over the threshold, and onto the balcony. Below, box hedges and a knot garden.

Beyond the knot garden, a rectangular, aqua-tiled pool. She sees herself diving, her fingertips parting a cluster of fallen leaves as she breaks the water's surface. Her arms pulling, her legs pushing, creating her own wake.

MALMAISON

She imagines it as if it were a newsreel. Jackie Kennedy, stepping out of a bullet-shaped Citroën in front of Malmaison, with the French Minister of Culture, Andre Malraux, beside her. It is May 1961. Only a week ago, Malraux's two sons died in a car crash, but yesterday, when Jackie expressed interest in visiting Empress Josephine's famous rose gardens at Malmaison, he decided to take her himself.

Malraux, author of *Man's Fate*, is a knowledgeable guide. As they tour the chateau, Jackie asks thought-provoking questions. He replies as a man would after the bottom has just dropped out of his life, the echo of a question in every answer.

By the time they enter the garden, she imagines the cameras are no longer with them. They pause beside a double gallica rose—a rose that Jackie recognizes from a Redouté painting that once hung in her grandmother's bedroom. Here, beside this rose's gray-green foliage, a staff of neatly uniformed gardeners materializes. One gardener steps forward, bearing a hand-tied arrangement of *Souvenir de la Malmaison* roses. As Jackie grasps the stems, her index finger and thumb disappear within the shadow beneath the bouquet's full-blown canopy and quiver for an instant, as if that darkness held a corner of her own black veil.

She takes a moment to compose herself, bending her face over the flowers. Inhaling. As she lifts her eyes, a smile forms on her lips. Malraux takes her bouquet. She steps forward, shaking the hand of each gardener, thanking each of them in turn. When Malraux returns the bouquet to her, she frees one stem and returns that single stem to him. In her precise yet flowing French—as if she is trying to convince herself as well as Malraux—she says, "My mother-in-law says that birds sing after a storm; why shouldn't people feel as free to delight in whatever remains to them?"

Then she turns to the gardeners. "Her name is Rose. Good that I should think of her here."

In the back seat of the Citroën on the forty-five-minute ride back to Paris, what do Jackie and Malraux speak of, as the *Souvenir de la Malmaison* roses on the seat between them offer a fountain of heady scent?

LODGED BETWEEN HER SHOULDER BLADES

At five o'clock, the Frenchwoman she dreams of leaves work, stops to pick up olives, small rounds of goat cheese, lettuces, and a baguette. When she gets home, she places the groceries on the kitchen counter beside the sink, showers, and changes into comfortable clothes. As she zips her jeans and pulls on a T-shirt, she thinks about winter's residue, a chill, coiled and lodged between her shoulder blades. This chill makes her think of the first roses, iceberg white, blooming early because they are planted beside a garden wall, a wall situated to collect the sun's heat all afternoon.

She walks outside into the garden and follows a path of circular stones to the flowers she has been thinking of. She presses the full length of her back and outstretched arms between the rosebush and the wall, delicately edging her way in, to avoid the thorns. At the first touch of warmth, she curls into herself and slides down the wall until her forehead rests on her knees and she is hidden behind the roses.

PARALLEL TO THE EARTH

An eighteenth-century Provençal chateau dominates the background of this landscape. A field of wheat spreads out in the foreground. The muted green stalks fade at the top to a shade only slightly more yellow than the chateau's walls.

A woman walks through this field. Her hair frames her face, pixie-style. She wears a sleeveless sheath, yellow linen of a shade even more muted than the chateau's walls. As she walks, she holds her hands outstretched, palms parallel to the earth, brushing the tips of the grain she walks through. In her imagination, she is walking through a field of feathers the same color as the wheat. The feathers graze her hands and legs. As she takes one step after the other, she begins to feel as if she may disappear, the way the color of the grain disappears at the tip of each shaft.

OPPOSITE DESIRE

A train station in Bordeaux. She stands on the platform. Her son, age four, holds one hand; her daughter, age six, holds the other.

Her son tugs to the left and says, "Toilet." Her daughter tugs to the right and says, "Ice cream."

The train whistle partially swallows their voices, but she knows what they want and smiles. It is August. After a summer of train rides to the beach and back, her children know this station well.

The toilets are to the left; the ice cream vendor is to the right. Ice cream, toilet. Toilet, ice cream. *Toilet first*, she decides, *then the ice cream*. In this moment, the priority is obvious. But so often their needs arise simultaneously, tugging her in opposite directions, as if a current ran through her body from her son's hand to his sister's. His need somehow triggers the opposite desire in her. Will it always be this way—push, pull?

Her son prefers going into the toilet stall alone, so she and her daughter wait by the sinks. They watch women come and go, soaping hands, knotting scarves, checking smiles or teeth in the mirror.

When one woman pulls out a crimson lipstick, she begins to imagine a different time—a woman with a cinched waist, flaring skirt over crinoline, high heels. The coveted fifties silhouette. Dior named them "flower women." This one with her Everest cheekbones and her hooded eyes looks into the mirror, but she's not telling what she knows.

TWIRL

She looks in the mirror as she adjusts the tilt of her wide-brimmed sun hat and remembers the freedom of traveling alone. In her memory, she is nineteen and lost in Lyon, her face half-hidden under the hat she bought a week before in Cannes because its wide straw brim said summer to her.

She's been following her nose all morning. No guidebook. No map. She's just followed it to the *fleuriste*, to the *fromagerie*, and to the *parfumerie*. Though now, for some reason, without the scent of anything guiding her, she leaves the late morning sunlight and walks beneath a stone arch into this pedestrian passageway. Groundwater, she thinks, before the dampness like cool hands on her body even registers.

Forward or back?

Forward. In minutes, the passageway leads to a courtyard. Light again. Seventeenth-century houses on all sides. A fountain in the center, where a boy and girl sail boats no bigger than matchboxes. Their mother sits beside them, trailing her fingers in the water.

She twirls on the cobblestones. Her skirt flares out. One hand holds her hat. Being lost in Lyon is more like being tipsy than being drunk. The boy and girl momentarily abandon their boats and twirl with her.

Suddenly, the smell of garlic. A restaurant nearby? Is it too early for lunch?

POOLING BENEATH IT

Sunday in Burgundy, Dijon, light like spun honey streams in through the windows. You can almost hear the bees in it.

A dinner table. A family. A walnut cutting board crowned with a whole roasted chicken, rivulets of juice pooling beneath it. Her husband stands at the head of the table, lifts the carving tools, fork in one hand, knife in the other; he pauses, collects attention—his own, his family's. His children's hands migrate to their laps, rest palms up. Her hands settle, too, as she stops wondering if the soufflé will rise.

Her husband smiles at his family, knows that, in a changing world, this carving ritual may rest a bit awkwardly on his children's shoulders, like a business suit rarely worn. When he was a boy, only sons were taught how to carve at the table, but he teaches his daughter, too. No one had to tell him to do this. He works in currencies. Changing values fascinate him.

He carves half of the bird, fanning out the breast meat on one side of a white platter, thigh and drumstick on the other. He touches the platter's rim for a moment, thinking of how his wife warmed it in the oven, then he steps back. His teenage daughter walks to the head of the table. She takes up the carving tools.

A long pause as she gathers her far-flung self, gathers her family to her. In this pause, she imagines Sunday dinner in her own family home when she is an adult. Light streams in through the windows. Her husband, children, and parents are seated on one side of the dining room table. Her brother and his family are seated across from them. All the children are young, fidgety, but she does it anyway, takes the long pause because, in her family, the prayer is the silence.

As she pauses, she imagines a eucalyptus grove in California near the coast, a sanctuary for migrating monarch butterflies. If you stand silent and perfectly still, hundreds of butterflies will land on your shoulders and outstretched arms.

In that moment, it comes to her: *Let my children dream of Monterey, of San Francisco, of the Rocky Mountains, of Milan, of Mumbai, of Sri Lanka, of the Tyrrhenian Sea, and the Gulf of Corinth. Let them dream of their own children, soft as baby owls nestled beside them. Let the herbs with which I baste give their lives richness and texture. Let warmth and resilience reside within them when they venture to the places they dream of.*

In her imagination, she touches *la chouette*, the owl, icon of Dijon, sculpted on the side of the Notre-Dame church. She touches it with her left hand as she passes from left to right beneath it, touches it so that her wish will be granted, as the legend promises.

LUMBERING BODY

Driving. Carnac. Fields of menhirs—standing stones—on either side of the road. She's running late for a doctor's appointment, one of several this week. As she presses the accelerator, the pain spikes from ankle, to knee, to the small of her back. The snake appears again in her imagination. Its X-marked, diamond-shaped head rests against the inside of the passenger window, looking out. Its body loops across the back seat, then curls over her left shoulder, tail tip resting on her jugular notch. Every time it exhales, she feels that tip pressing deeper into the notch.

In her imagination, she stops the car, opens the Peugeot door, watches the snake's great lumbering body zigzag away from the asphalt, across the grass, faster than you would expect. Making a beeline. Coiling round a rooted, sun-backed stone.

It always chooses a stone far from the road, a stone deep-lined like the palm of a hand. When she watches it coil, she is certain the snake must be grateful for each of its vertebrae.

SHAKES HER FIST

Alone in Calais. Walking. First light. No one in the world knows where she is.

She stops in front of a shop, near the *place du Soldat Inconnu*, staring through plate glass at a window display of running shoes heaped beside a mannequin that wears jogging shorts and sits cross-legged, peering into an empty gym locker. Just above the jogger's head, she notices the statue's filmy reflection, six robed men, dark but glinting.

She does a one-eighty, jaywalks across the empty street, slides onto a night-chilled granite bench, lets her tote slouch almost open-mouthed on the bench beside her. Inhale. Exhale. She looks up at the statue, thinks of Rodin's hands.

Anyone watching would notice her taut shoulders and straight back, the defined muscles in her forearms, her ropy calves. They might expect the camera and water bottle in her tote, but they would probably be surprised by the handmade journal, and how she knew to use a classic embroidery stitch on the binding so that, today, when she opens the journal, both sides lie flat on her lap and she can write on one side without the pages on the other side fanning up as if the book is continually trying to fold itself back together over her hand.

She is about to satisfy a promise she made to herself after her sister's death: Record each dream, in sequence, named and numbered.

Calais, Dream # 13.
A moss-covered well, a woman beside it. A figure descends, offers the woman wings or the book in his hands. The downdraft frightens her so she takes the book. She wants to shake her fist, holler, "These are not the choices I want. You. You. Stop sending them." But it would only tire her.

She presses the book to her chest. Stubbornness corkscrews through her.

She looks up, envies the Burghers the strength that Rodin put into their limbs. She wants to lift the nooses from their necks, touch their legs to life and say, "Let's sprint on the beach to the green-hatted cliffs. What deep footprints you'll leave in the sand."

REINVENTS ITSELF

She knows that anyone else seeing this lavender field in Provence would be haunted by the color of the flowers, which are purple, really, more saturated than anything she would think of as lavender, becoming lavender only after a long time hung upside down in a dark, cool place to dry.

But instead of the color, she is haunted by the shape of the bushes, each bush a rounded dome. This curved line reinvents itself in her imagination. She sees fields of half-moons, half-melons, half-peaches, half-plums, purple again across the earth's own arching surface.

SCRAWLED ON THE BLACKBOARD

Junior high school. She sits in the last row of desks at the back of the room. Everything in the front of the room blurs, including the teacher's face and the images on the video her seventh grade French class is watching.

Because she cannot actually see the images on the screen, she begins to invent scenes to go with the dialogue. She dreams up faces for the characters, *Mon Oncle* and his nieces. She imagines street corners where they can linger, asking directions. *Où est la bibliothèque? Où est le Mont Saint-Michel?*

This French class has no textbook. All of the information is meant to come from the video she can't see and from the teacher's blurry indecipherable notes scrawled on the chalkboard.

When midterm grades come out, her parents are alarmed. She has an eye exam, glasses are prescribed, and, at her parents' request, she is moved to a seat at the front of the room where she can no longer project her own images of France across the screen and the teacher's face, which is now vivid and three-dimensional.

She sees *Mon Oncle* and his nieces for the first time. They are certainly attractive, but not as she had imagined them. The *bibliothèque* is larger than she expected. Mont Saint-Michel is beautiful.

OUT BETWEEN THEM

She remembers pedaling, following her brother over the freshly paved roads of suburbia. When it was too hot to ride bikes, they'd spread a puzzle out between them on his bedroom floor. Their grandmother got them started on the big puzzles—not puzzles of ponies or dogs, but a puzzle of Degas's dancers. The one where the white-haired ballet master stands to the side, hands resting on his shoulder-high staff. The ballerinas scattered around him stretch or rest or chew their nails. Their mothers wait at the far end of the room.

That first big puzzle, that was the one where her brother taught her how to find the corners first, then the edges, and fill in the center last. He said, "With this many pieces, you have to have a system."

He was right about that. The system was efficient. But after a few days of working on that puzzle, her sweaty legs sticking to the hardwood floor, she began to long for a different puzzle, one with a blank box top, no picture to convey the whole. She wanted the piece at the exact center of that puzzle to come in a little cellophane pouch. She wanted to start with that piece and build from the center out.

BARE FEET

The night of her father's death, she dreams that they are together in France, standing beside enormous French doors, looking out. In the distance, she sees an armillary sphere centered in a perfectly square knot garden. Just beyond the door, a sprawling lacecap hydrangea is partially visible. Its milky petals echo the moon. Her desire to see the pale violet at the center of each flower is almost unbearable.

She and her father stand together at the door, but he does not take the handle. She knows she cannot turn it for him. The room is suddenly cold. She looks down at their bare feet, side by side on the stone floor, and remembers how the likeness of their feet fascinated her when she was a child. When she looks up, a cloaked, hooded figure stands on the other side of the door. He holds a lantern in one hand, and opens the door into the garden with the other. "Hermes," she says.

This word nudges her father's memory, and she sees the sudden recognition in his eyes as he grasps the meaning of a text read long ago. He crosses the threshold, and she is left alone at the open doorway. The fragrance of jasmine rushes in to cover her.

COUNTESS OLENSKA

She imagines a curator working at the Palais Galliera, the Fashion Museum of the City of Paris. Her workroom is filled with mannequins—almost-porcelain, featureless women, dressed in *Haute Couture*. The curator is at her desk, studying a Jeanne Lanvin evening dress on a mannequin across the room. A dress designed in the summer of 1923.

She has been trying to write a description of Lanvin's dress for a catalogue. She can't quite get it right, so she begins again. Silver lamé, ombré ribbon in red, pink, blue, green, and chartreuse. Floral embroidery. Blue satin. Seed pearls. Silver gauze. Signature "Lanvin blue" looped train. Egret feathers. It sounds like something that escaped from a zoo or from a mind incapable of editing itself, yet the dress is as quiet as a Chopin berceuse.

She begins again. Writing catalogue descriptions is not her favorite part of the job. But she is happy because the museum has finally agreed to her proposal to put these clothes on living women—the only way to understand what these designers were capable of.

Her plea to the director, "All these dresses were made to be worn, and to be worn is to move." As she says this, her arms glide in an abbreviated breaststroke—she hopes in a good imitation of a flowing skirt. "The full genius of such gowns is only revealed when a woman crosses a room in one of them, like Countess Olenska in *The Age of Innocence*. That's when you see the outline of a thigh beneath bias cut silk or the light rippling back and forth between folds of a paneled skirt."

The curator tells the director, "The models who wear these dresses will tell the story of wearing them to their children and grandchildren. That is how we keep history alive."

CARNELIAN STRIPED

A seamstress in Amiens stands at an upstairs bedroom window. Her hair is swept back, secured with a strip of multi-colored fabric. She leans out, pushing open the folding casement window, a two-handed, two-armed gesture. The second-story breeze swirls a few tendrils of gray hair across her face.

Not an aerial view, but something akin to it, as she contemplates the parrot tulips and remembers the day she first saw them in the Dutch bulb catalogue. Their hybrid name, *Dionysus*, in bold beside their picture. Such a pattern, she'd thought, yolky and carnelian striped, so like a pair of bell-bottom pants she cherished in the 1970s.

Later today, after lunch, when she is bent over, weeding, the fringed corollas of these tulips will brush her forearms, reminding her of a painter, her first wild-haired love, and a time when she kissed the place on his hand between the thumb and first finger, the place where a paintbrush often rested.

DOWNPOUR EXPECTED

Calais. Refugee Camp. The cardboard box filled with rain ponchos is heavy. She sets it down on a makeshift table, a plank resting on two stones. Instead of handing out the plastic ponchos, one for you, one for you, one for you, as if they were bottles of water and not garments, she gestures for the women gathered around her to each come forward and select her own.

The women hesitate. Then they approach the box one at a time, and look inside. Red ponchos, green ponchos, pink flowered ponchos. Women surround her now, taking the ponchos out of their plastic wrappers, lifting the ponchos over each other's heads. Women wearing red, and green, and a flower-power pink print like the one Twiggy wore on the cover of *Seventeen* magazine in the sixties.

An elderly woman, wearing one of the flowered ponchos, walks toward her, takes her hand, squeezes. She can feel the bone in it.

BREASTBONE

Her eyes open as she wakes from a dream. The fluorescent glow of her digital clock is somehow both pleasing and irritating as it displays the answer even before the question is fully formed—6:00 a.m.

She closes her eyes and burrows beneath the covers. The dream comes back to her.

A clearing. The French countryside. Two drifters, or two poachers, or Vladimir and Estragon escaped from Beckett, finally, sitting cross-legged beside the campfire's banked embers as they view the charred remains of a rabbit's stripped breastbone, its ribs open to the sky.

The shadowy figures, whoever they are, drifters or poachers or characters fled from a play, smile and recline, the rabbit's flesh within them now, where the hunger was.

TOWARD

She is resting on a bench in the Jardin des Tuileries, daydreaming about Hephaestus, a god thrust out of heaven by his mother or his father—no one is quite sure which, because the myths run in both directions. Hephaestus, rescued by the sea nymphs, Thetis and Eurynome, then nurtured underwater for nine years. Hephaestus, a fiery, smoldering god, an incarnation of the Roman god Vulcan, who emerges from the watery depths reborn as artist, craftsman, metallurgist, and keeper of the forge.

She wants Thetis and Eurynome to come and claim her, take all the fire within her to some watery underworld, so she can live submerged with creatures that drift and undulate, then emerge with bits of seaweed clinging to her thighs and arms, her eyes a new blue, Mediterranean, the color they were when she was a child standing in full sun.

But what then, she asks herself, *what happens after the moment of transformation?*

She thinks of Hephaestus again; imagines him beside the forge; imagines his muscular back, his blackened hands, his clubfeet; and Aphrodite, his exquisite, unfaithful wife, standing beside him. She knows the rest of the story, sees it stretched out like fabric across a loom. She knows Hephaestus will one day devise nets to capture his wife and Ares, one of her many lovers. She knows this vengeance will bring him no joy.

Perhaps it is better to sit beside these long-stemmed tulips, known throughout the world as *French* tulips, rather than risk the watery depths. Today the tulip beds sway like kelp on currents of air instead of water. Perhaps this is enough.

FRAMING AND REFRAMING

At the back of the amphitheater, a wall of arches rises up, framing and reframing an endless blue sky. In the curve of each arch she sees a line that extends upward and then descends, an architectural detail that expresses yearning for both heaven and earth. In her dreams of France, the fragment of the Roman amphitheater holds a special place, here, where so much of the original structure remains.

Today, she dreams a *jeune femme* is walking up the hillside behind the theater. As she walks, the young woman anticipates the wild crocus along the path and moves slowly so she can savor their newness and her own grace, each foot lifted and returned to the earth. She is so young. She does not ask herself what makes a favorite walk a favorite, does not think about how easily she breathes, despite the climb. Instead, she thinks about Dire Straits, Metallica, and Depeche Mode—about the musicians who have all swung their hair, stamped their feet and shaken their hips in this theater.

When the path emerges at the top of the hill, it winds through a square park, past bay laurels, an empty fountain and a few benches where the moss has made inroads over the carved anthemion. Two women wearing almost-identical striped spandex dresses and layers of makeup sit on one of the benches, consulting a guidebook, chatting as they go back and forth between the view of the Roman theater and the pictures of it in the book. As they point out details, their fluttering red nails remind her of the markings on blackbirds' wings, appearing and disappearing with each gesture.

These women seem older than she is, by several years, and she wonders if their pleasure in the theater is an escape from jobs that are mundane and repetitive. She cannot imagine why they climbed the hill in high heels, but when they laugh, the sound of their pleasure increases her own.

At last, she reaches her favorite bench, the one closest to the edge. If she had ever lived in a city, she might think about how this spot resembles a rooftop, but she has never made her way up in an elevator and stepped out onto a skyscraper's observation deck, so for her this moment is singular, experienced without contrast or comparison.

The Romans had no way of knowing their theater would endure, would still be in use centuries beyond their own imaginations, would remain. The rising stone arches seem to intensify the sky's blue. When she looks up, beyond the stage, through the stone arches, she feels herself to be a creature without age or gender, without body or country, as transparent as the air she breathes.

*It is not what France gave you but what it
did not take away from you that was important.*

—Gertrude Stein

ACKNOWLEDGMENTS

My gratitude to the editors of *New Millennium Writings, Bitter Oleander, Paterson Literary Review, Laurel Review, Cloudbank, The Round, American Mustard,* and *Unstitched States,* where versions of some of these poems first appeared.

Thanks to friends, family, and my writing group for their continual goodwill and inspiration. Thanks to those who helped shape the manuscript: Molly Giles, an early reader; Bill Mohr, who helped me expand it; Gretchen Henderson, who helped me trim it; and Cecilia Woloch, who helped me find the book's final form. Their enthusiasm and honesty were essential.

There are several teachers I would like to thank: Monika Wikman, an artful guide through the imaginal realms; Ellen Sheffield and Gretchen Henderson, for creating The Art of Text at Kenyon College; Bill Mohr, for organizing The Poet's Metamorphosis; and finally Diane di Prima and David Meltzer, who were there at the beginning.

Thanks to my most able and trustworthy assistant Dorrit Geshuri, whose hands took over the keyboard for me when I broke my wrist. A special thanks to *New Millennium Writings* for awarding "Bougainvillea" their 2016 Poetry Prize.

Most of all, thanks to Blue Light Press for the Blue Light Book Award, their decision to publish this book, and their patience as I worked to complete it.

CPSIA information can be obtained
at www.ICGtesting.com
Printed in the USA
FSOW01n1553130218
44416FS